# WHEN YOUR FRIEND IS SCARED

BY ALLAN MOREY

BLUE OWL BOOKS

# TIPS FOR CAREGIVERS

Social and emotional learning (SEL) helps children grow their self and social awareness. They will learn how to manage their emotions and foster empathy toward others. Lessons and support in SEL help children build relationship skills, establish positive habits in communication and cooperation, and make better decisions. By incorporating SEL in early reading, children will have the opportunity to explore different emotions, as well as learn ways to cope with theirs and those of others.

## BEFORE READING

Talk to the reader about fear. Explain that it is an emotion everyone experiences.

**Discuss:** How do you feel when you are afraid? How do you react? Do you notice other people reacting the same way? Do your friends share some of the same fears?

## AFTER READING

Talk to the reader about how to recognize when someone else is scared.

**Discuss:** How can you talk to a friend who is afraid? What should you do and say to help a friend overcome his or her fears?

## SEL GOAL

Young students struggle to understand their own emotions, and it can be even more difficult for them to recognize how someone else is feeling. Being able to spot clues in a friend's body language and actions will help improve their social awareness skills. Lead students in a discussion about how they react to something that scares them. By sharing this information with each other, students can learn how to communicate with a friend or peer who might be feeling scared.

# TABLE OF CONTENTS

# CHAPTER 1

# RECOGNIZING FEAR

How do we look when we are scared? Our eyes open wide. We raise our eyebrows. Our nostrils **flare**. Some people even open their mouths wide.

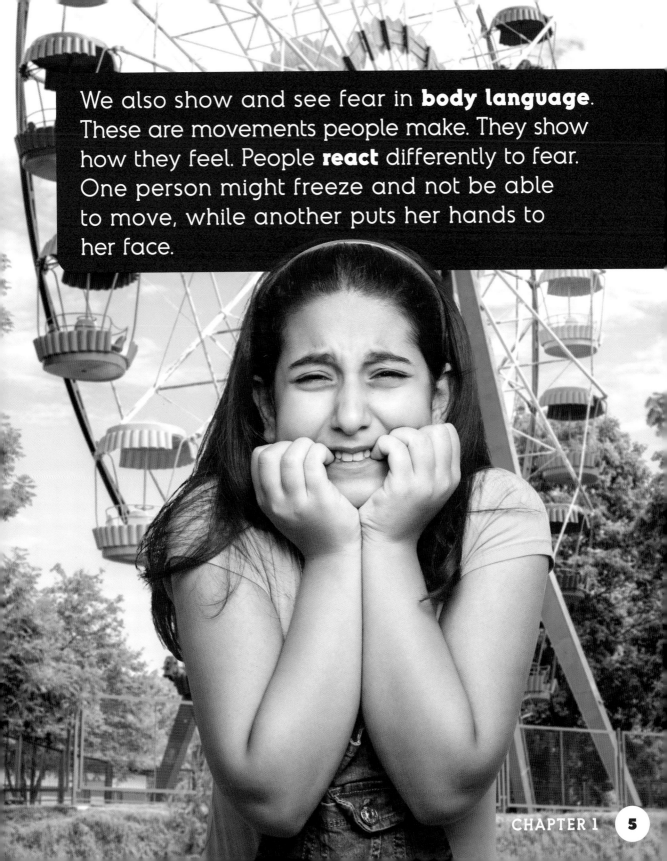

We also show and see fear in **body language**. These are movements people make. They show how they feel. People **react** differently to fear. One person might freeze and not be able to move, while another puts her hands to her face.

Does your body **tremble** when you are afraid? Or get **tense**? Gina screams when she is **startled**. Another friend **gasps**. Another jumps. They can't control it!

## FIGHT OR FLIGHT

Fear can cause a **fight-or-flight response**. When a big bug buzzes about, one friend might swat at it. Another friend might run from it. These responses are meant to protect us from harm.

Fear makes some people sweat. Ty is afraid of flying in an airplane. His heart beats fast. He breathes faster, too. He doesn't feel sick, but some people do when they're this scared!

## DID YOU KNOW?

A **phobia** is a very extreme fear. Being afraid to fly in airplanes is a common phobia. So is being afraid of the dark. Other common phobias include a fear of crowded spaces and a fear of being alone.

# CHAPTER 2

# UNDERSTANDING FEAR

We all get scared for different reasons. That can make it difficult to understand why others are afraid. Think. How do you feel when you are scared? This can help you understand someone else's feelings.

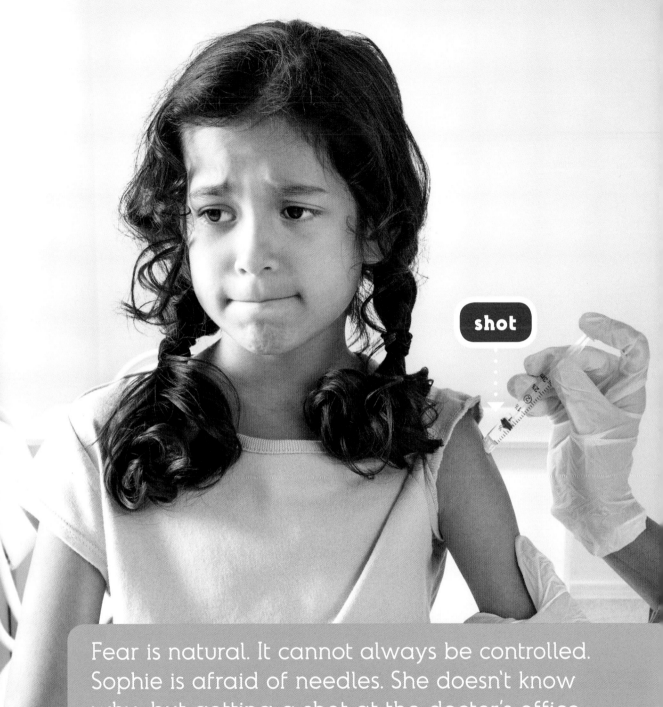

shot

Fear is natural. It cannot always be controlled. Sophie is afraid of needles. She doesn't know why, but getting a shot at the doctor's office scares her.

Some people like being scared! It can be fun to feel **suspense**, like when we ride roller coasters, watch scary movies, or walk through haunted houses around Halloween.

Our hearts beat fast, but these are all safe. So the fear can feel exciting!

Some fears cause **anxiety**. Joe gets anxious before taking a test because he's afraid he won't do well. Another friend might be afraid of standing up in front of class. He gets so nervous he can't speak.

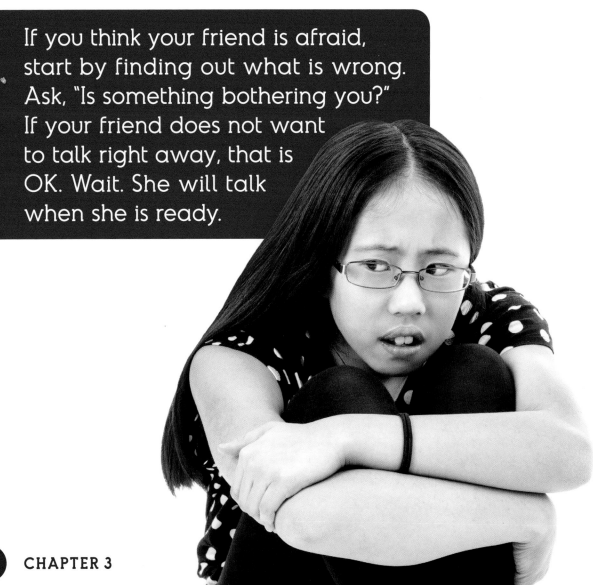

# CHAPTER 3

# RESPONDING TO FEAR

If you think your friend is afraid, start by finding out what is wrong. Ask, "Is something bothering you?" If your friend does not want to talk right away, that is OK. Wait. She will talk when she is ready.

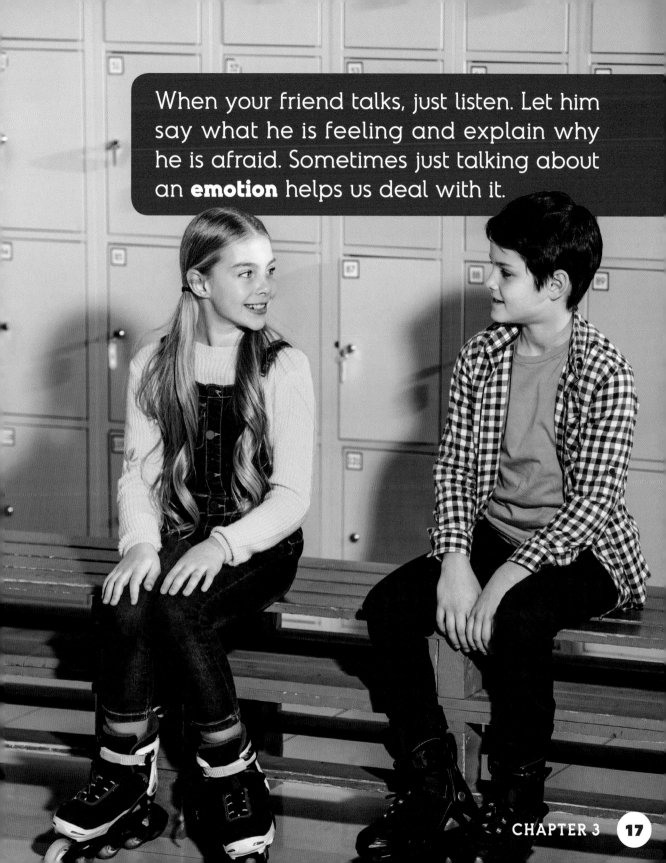

When your friend talks, just listen. Let him say what he is feeling and explain why he is afraid. Sometimes just talking about an **emotion** helps us deal with it.

Support your friend. Is she afraid of dogs? Tell her you understand her fear. Don't tease her about it or say her fear is silly. That could make her feel worse. Instead, ask her what she finds scary about dogs. Maybe in time she will feel comfortable meeting your dog!

## OVERCOMING FEAR

If we **avoid** our fears, they can seem even scarier. But facing your fears might help you overcome them. Are you afraid of spiders? Learn more about them! Knowing more about something can help us understand it. Then we are less likely to be afraid of it.

Ask how you can help. Is your friend afraid of being in front of the class? Let him practice talking in front of you.

Helping a friend is **rewarding**. Your friend will feel better. You will feel good, too! Talking to a friend about his fear may even help you understand your own fears. What will you do the next time your friend is afraid?

# GOALS AND TOOLS

## GROW WITH GOALS

Everyone gets scared for different reasons. How can you help yourself and your friends overcome fears?

**Goal:** Write down something you are afraid of. Then write down what about it scares you. How does your body and mind feel when you are afraid?

**Goal:** Face your fears! Confront your fears by trying something that scares you. You might realize it wasn't scary at all. You might even find you like it!

**Goal:** Help a friend overcome a fear! Facing a fear with someone else could help your friend face that fear!

## WRITING REFLECTION

With a friend, write down all of the things that both of you are afraid of.

1. What fears do you share? Why do you think you have some of the same fears?

2. For the fears that are yours, try to explain what about them scares you.

3. How do you feel after talking about your fears?

**anxiety**
A feeling of worry or fear.

**avoid**
To stay away from something or to try to prevent something from happening.

**body language**
The gestures, movements, and mannerisms by which people communicate with others.

**emotion**
A feeling, such as happiness, anger, or sadness.

**fight-or-flight response**
To either prepare to defend oneself or run when faced with something scary.

**flare**
To widen, as in a person's nostrils.

**gasps**
Breathes in suddenly because of surprise, pain, or exercise.

**phobia**
An extremely strong fear.

**react**
To behave in a particular way as a response to something that has happened.

**rewarding**
Offering or bringing satisfaction.

**startled**
Surprised, frightened, or alarmed, causing a quick, involuntary movement.

**suspense**
An anxious or uncertain feeling caused by not knowing what might happen next.

**tense**
Stretched stiff and tight.

**tremble**
To shake in a way one can't control, especially from cold, fear, or excitement.

## TO LEARN MORE

**FACT SURFER**

## Finding more information is as easy as 1, 2, 3.

1. Go to www.factsurfer.com

2. Enter "**whenyourfriendisscared**" into the search box.

3. Choose your cover to see a list of websites.

# INDEX

Blue Owl Books are published by Jump!, 5357 Penn Avenue South, Minneapolis, MN 55419, www.jumplibrary.com

Library of Congress Cataloging-in-Publication Data

Names: Morey, Allan, author.
Title: When your friend is scared / by Allan Morey.
Description: Blue Owl books edition. | Minneapolis, MN: Jump!, Inc., 2020. | Series: You've got a friend
Includes index. | Audience: Ages 7–10. | Audience: Grades 2–3.
Identifiers: LCCN 2019033957 (print)
LCCN 2019033958 (ebook)
ISBN 9781645272212 (paperback)
ISBN 9781645272205 (hardcover)
ISBN 9781645272229 (ebook)
Subjects: LCSH: Fear–Juvenile literature. | Fear in children–Juvenile literature.
Friendship–Juvenile literature.
Classification: LCC BF575.F2 M688 2020 (print)
LCC BF575.F2 (ebook) | DDC 152.4/6–dc23
LC record available at https://lccn.loc.gov/2019033957
LC ebook record available at https://lccn.loc.gov/2019033958

Editor: Susanne Bushman
Designer: Molly Ballanger

Photo Credits: Oleg Golovnev/EyeEm/Getty, cover; Mark Nazh/Shutterstock, 1; stanfram/iStock, 3; Dean Drobot/Shutterstock, 4; Khosrork/iStock, 5 (foreground); Dmirti Ma/Shutterstock, 5 (background); CREATISTA/Shutterstock, 6–7; kitisak pingkasarn/Shutterstock, 8–9 (foreground); keellla/Shutterstock, 8–9 (background); PeopleImages/iStock, 10; Terry Vine/Getty, 11; kali9/iStock, 12–13; Lisa F. Young/Shutterstock, 14–15; ronniechua/iStock, 16; LightField Studios/Shutterstock, 17; ER Productions Limited/Getty, 18–19; Wavebreakmedia/iStock, 20–21.

Printed in the United States of America at Corporate Graphics in North Mankato, Minnesota.